The Dark Honey

The Dark Honey

◎ ◎ ◎ ◎ ◎

New & Used Poems

Ellie Schoenfeld

Clover Valley Press, LLC
Duluth, Minnesota

Clover Valley Press, LLC
6286 Homestead Rd.
Duluth, MN 55804-9621
USA

Cover design by Stacie Whaley, i.e. design
Cover image © iStockphoto.com: Dimco Photography

Printed in the United States of America on acid-free paper.

Library of Congress Control Number: 2009924939

ISBN-10: 0-9794883-5-4
ISBN-13: 978-0-9794883-5-1

Acknowledgments

Many of these poems previously appeared in the following publications: *Northcoast Review, Poetry Motel, Runes, Loonfeather, Poets Who Haven't Moved to Minneapolis* (Poetry Harbor, 1990), *Poets Who Haven't Moved to St. Paul* (Poetry Harbor, 1992), *Mondo Barbie* (St. Martin's Press, 1993), *Thirteen Broadsides* (Tweed Museum: The Press, 1995), *Café au Lake* (1998), *Screaming Red Gladiolus!* (Poetry Harbor, 1999), *Difficult Valentines* (Fallow Deer Books, 2003), *The Moon Rolls Out of Our Mouths* (Calyx Press, 2005), *North Country Sampler* (Calyx Press, 2005), *Response* (Calyx Press, 2006), *To Sing Along the Way* (New Rivers Press, 2006), *Getting to Maybe* (Randon House Canada, 2006), *Erotic Justice* (Calyx Press, 2007), and *Trail Guide* (Calyx Press, 2008). Recordings of some may be found on the collaborative CDs: *Personal Ad* (2000), *Almost Through the Rinse Cycle* (2006), and *Taking It Off (2008).*

2016
Merry Christmas
Aunt Anne!
Sending warm thoughts
of sitting by the fire
and reading good
poetry together. All
our love and hugs!
Annie, Tanaki,
& Truman

In loving memory of
Esther Nahgahnub and Alex Smith

Contents

◎ TWO

◎ THREE

◎ FOUR

◉ ONE

Never assume the obvious is true.

— William Saffire

SOMETIMES

Sometimes the confines
become just too much.
Too much to keep remembering
to keep track of which lines
we should and should not
cross. Sometimes
the compartments
won't stay tidy—one thing
seeps into another, things mix
in unexpected ways, transform.
We cannot always control alchemy.
Sometimes you are eating
something with rhubarb
and the coffee spills
and an image of Mary or Jesus appears,
your quiet kitchen table
instantly converted
to a shrine, your house
filled with the faithful, your life
suddenly on a course
you had never considered before. ◉

READY OR NOT

after a print by Joe Shores, *say when to say when (not yet)*

All of it is inevitable.
The fierce heat of living
illuminates the landscapes of our lives,
the holy ground littered
with almost unrecognizable tinder,
the broken glass of forgotten bottles.

Every morning the sun
sets the world on fire.
The world, a giant jack pine seed,
which can only germinate
after some sort of conflagration, an intercourse
of chaotic terror and terrible beauty.
With every slant of light
the remembered world shifts.

Even the watery moon
is full of fire.
There are times she blazes orange and opulent,
the sensual, unpredictable mouth of Etna,
wild and wide open,
spewing songs that stir something
deep and hidden and almost forgotten.
The breath of her singing
ignites embers and inner immolations.

Everything everywhere
burns and is born anew
in the insistent and abundant
generosity of light.
Every morning
the sun rises.
Every evening,
the moon. ◉

DECIPHERING THE LANGUAGE OF FIRE

The dark erotic nuances of blue—
its caverns, its secrets.

The enthusiasms of orange.

The nouns in the embers—
a litany of names
who quench my restlessness.

Unknowable messages of sparks
transform into something
invisible, essential,
the purest of poems.

The iambic pentameter of flames,
the way the rhythms inform
my pulse. I try to sing along,

to let my body undulate and sway,
let it be carried,
let it ignite.

My body speaks
in its original language
of water and earth.

I open my mouth
and a river of paper flowers
flows into the light. ◉

NAKED WITH THE LEOPARDS

When I close my eyes
it is not February,
I am not in Duluth
and these women in concert
with their drums
along with the rest of us
are in Kenya.
It is warm
and we are dancing
in the sunlight
until Zuni is talking something
about night runners
who run naked with the leopards
so now it is night
and I have added a large fire,
subtracted our clothes.
Leopard eyes flash at the edges.
There is a distracting moment
when I think, "Even if it was warm here
there would be mosquitoes and what kinds
of insects live in Kenya?"
I concentrate on returning
to the circle, notice
that I have given myself
a different body,
thin and muscular.

I roll my eyes and add a few pounds,
remove that muscle tone, those cheekbones.
The varicose veins and cellulite
take a whole extra song
but finally they too
join the dance
and when the applause arrives
I have stopped flinching.
The real me sweats and laughs
then runs to the forest,
vanishes with the leopards. ◉

INTERVIEW WITH GOD

In the dream I am a journalist who has landed an interview with God and God is a wrinkly old man wearing an aqua tutu. He can tell that I am a little surprised by His appearance, says He picked the god as a human male thing to match my upbringing, and the tutu (which I don't remember hearing anything about while growing up) well, He confesses that it has always surprised Him that humans, who have free will and can wear anything they like, don't all just gravitate to ballet clothes. Those lushly colored, diaphanous fabrics which lend themselves to twirling—an activity God suggests we spend more time in—are one of the better things we have ever come up with. We discuss fabric for a while and then I ask Him if humans are really the most evolved of the species. He has a hearty belly laugh, tells me how much we crack Him up, pulls Himself together and tells me no. Says the raspberries, for example, are light years ahead of us. Think about it—there they are with their berries that perfect shade of red, that pleasing texture, they offer up their sweet sensuous selves to the world, they spread joy, don't argue, have flags, feel patriotic, or go to war. They just share their perfect selves and here God reminds me about the ones who were good enough to plant themselves right by where I park my earth-destroying car. They don't hold this car against me, they know that humans are not smart enough to do anything else. I ask about the sparkly crown which is more like a tiara and He says, yes, that's what it is because *tiara* is such a prettier word than *crown*, which implies kingdoms and that bad impulse to go to war whereas a shiny tiara just makes a man feel pretty. God laughs, says He thinks He was a crow in a past life and I think Wait! It's me who thinks this crow thing about themselves to explain my attraction to shiny objects, so maybe this is one of those lesson dreams, maybe I'm starting to think of myself as God when I should clearly be trying to emulate a raspberry and when I wake up I eat my new role model for breakfast because I have always heard that you are what you eat. ◉

8

BELLOWS

after a print by Nick Wroblewski, *Bellows of Our Shared Breath*

The clouds rise up,
soft bellows of our shared breath
fan the flames
of the earth's desires.
Red passions burn
where the sky strokes
the horizon.
Every morning
this consummation creates
a new day
into which every living thing
breathes life.
The clouds
whisper the stories of everything.
They hint at horses rearing
and whales breaching,
at the big picture
always shifting
in time
to

the steady beat
of

the first prayer—
an almost breathless

yes. ◙

PARTING THE RED SEA

My fingers swim
through red clay seas
that I am parting
to plant tulips.
The earth is cold
because I have waited
till the last minute.
I am thinking
this is an act of faith,
an affirmative to Einstein's question
"Is the universe a friendly place?"
Yes, except for the squirrels
who ate all Yvonne's bulbs
and she lives close to me.
She bought new ones
and soaked them in something
squirrels don't like.
She told me this
while there was still
ample time to learn
from her experience.
But I didn't soak these.
They are my prayers.
Last minute.

An on-the-edge reckless dare
I will take their growth
or demise as a sign,
a message either way
from the spirits
who are probably unimpressed
with the spiritual weight
with which I am sinking
these bulbs into the earth.
Spirits who could be dancing
in these maple leaves,
laughing at my solemn garden religion,
surfing through altars of mulch.
If someone asks me
what I believe in,
I say "tulips." ◎

STONES

after a print by Joel Cooper, *Cascade Cabin*

You keep a stone from the island
in your pocket,
hold it in your hands like a prayer,
place it under your pillow
like a talisman
who whispers stories to you in the night.
You keep one in your pocket
and under your pillow
until that day arrives

when you leave it
on the hearth
and walk out the door
for the final time.
You take one last look around
before you cross the hidden bridge
on the other side of the island.
You cross that bridge
which no one can see with these eyes
but which the rocks
have been quietly describing to you for years.
Your last breath here is
a sigh of relief,
a smoky prayer the stones taught you
while you were sleeping. ◉

NEW YEAR

An icy January night.
Snowflakes waltz under
the streetlight, unperturbed. Recently

another friend buried.
Ashes and dust and odd moments
from an incompletely remembered
questionable past
blow around at my feet,
random leaves
from the tree of life. Still

here in my room
everything is very quiet. Somewhere

deep underground
tulip bulbs stir ever so slightly,
whisper their voluptuous ideas
to the frozen earth. ◉

THE RAIN FALLS ON THE ROOF

The rain falls on the roof in Spanish.
Yesterday it was Italian,
day before that, Ojibway.
It falls in German
when it wants to be emphatic.
Sometimes the rain speaks languages
I don't recognize, can't quite put my finger on—
maybe one of those click ones from the Kalahari
or a prayer in some obscure dialect of Sanskrit,
the lexicon of the religion with the most gods.
Sometimes the rain speaks in tongues.

The rain is chatty, especially at night
when it can't sleep either.
It tells me the news
from the fish and the birds,
the gossip of the dragonflies.
It lets me know its true feelings
about snow and hail, monsoons and hurricanes,
the complexities of ice.
It spent its time
in the watertables of the earth,
in the rivers of the world
before rising into the arms of the clouds,
before returning to us,
to those of us who are so dry and thirsty for its stories.
In the vernacular of sugar maples,
it tells me about a song it learned
from a red leaf falling.

I know that it says all the same things
to all the neighbors, but I like to imagine
that it confides in me alone,
that I matter to the rain
in some small but essential way.
I like to believe that
when the rooftop conversation is over
and that when those drops and rivulets glide
agonizingly, erotically, slowly
down the window pane
in Russian or Hebrew or Spanish again,
they get translated into a secret language,
into very private and meaningful messages
only and specifically for me. ◉

ROOF

In my dream the roof
was giving way,
the corners of boxes
stored in the attic
starting to poke through
the ceiling—some sort of problem
that went unattended
for too long.
An avalanche was about to occur
yet no one seemed very alarmed.
I tried to warn them
but they wouldn't listen.
Eventually I woke up
saving only myself. ◉

SPRING 1999

The new blades of grass
slash through the recently exposed
vulnerable earth.
Even without the snow,
the mulch in the garden
at the bottom of the stairs
still holds the footprints
of the ambulance crew
as they carried you out of the house.
They tried to carry you out
into the February cold uncovered
but I covered you with the blanket you like
and sent it along on your final journey
because you told me you especially enjoyed
the gift of a blanket.
The new green and even a flower
are trying to push their way up
to the garish light
of these ever lengthening days.
If I don't pull off the mulch,
it will rot that new growth.
If I don't pull off the mulch,
the new green will
force itself up anyway.
It can't be stopped there is no going back
it doesn't matter what I do.
The buds explode on the trees,
the new blades of grass
just slice and slice. ◉

ALWAYS RETURNING

I am always returning to this body
of water, to this plot
of soil with its complicated characters
of sunflower and pine,
fungi and ferns.
Always returning
to the practice of watching
light move around a room,
contemplating the quality
of every shadow, the meaning
of the small currents
who nudge the curtains,
who carry the flecks of dust.
Flecks transformed
by the alchemy of sunlight
into diamonds, into secret messages
inside of invisible bottles
bobbing on invisible seas
always trying to return to shore. ◉

RED

Red ship waits
for the harbor.
Red sky
waits for the night. ◉

CALL

The foghorn and the ship
call to each other
in plaintive groans.
The crow outside my window
delivers a message.
I am sleeping still
between worlds, understanding
everything and nothing. ◉

AN ANSWER TO YOUR QUESTION

The moon is always
where you think she will be
except when she isn't.
The moon is spotlighting
a grave marker in Red Cliff,
shining on the ashes of Lew and Alex
as they swim through eternity
in the cold and deep of Lake Superior.
The moon waltzes every night
with our dearly departed,
she whispers rumors about us
in their ears and makes them laugh.
The moon is fond of gossip and jokes.

The moon understands and inspires
our particular brands of lunacy.
Every cell in our bloodstream, a tiny moon
full of light and madness.
She looks into our memories,
illuminates what we need to see,
gently shadows what we cannot bear.
The moon is one of the few entities
who never asks too much of us.
The moon can see every turn and nuance
of every strand of our DNA, she reads us
like a book of our best and worst poems.
The moon knows all of our secrets.

She gives us grandmotherly advice
which we rarely listen to
because we don't like to be told what to do
especially if it would be good for us.
The moon never leaves us
because of our flaws and frailties.

The moon sends shadow pictures to you
through the poplar trees,
she blinks messages to me
from the surface of the water.
The messages are of the utmost importance
and I rarely understand them.
I go on ignorant and crazy
all lit up by a waltzing light.
The moon hangs in the sky
above our houses.
The moon, she is inside of us.
The moon whispers in our ears
"Now you see me,
now you don't." ◉

FRAGMENTS

The pupil in my eye
wants to study you.

The grandmother sits
round and womanly and full
in the night sky.

In the dreams flecked grandfather stones
take on the shapes of hands and turtles.
I am riding a horse who ambles slowly
so I can watch the river path.

You never know more than half
of anyone else's story
even if they tell you
everything they know.

Despite what we are told
we never really know
whether it will rain or not
and there are days
where every step is an argument
about who will get to keep
the sandal.

The pupil in my eye
wants to study you.

It is winter and we are deer who are hungry.
We lick the salt of each other's wounds
without conclusions or summaries or hope.
We dream a dreamless sleep.

We are only here
for the blink of an eye.

The grandmother sits
round and womanly and full
in the night sky. ◉

LAUNDRY

If cleanliness is next to godliness
then doing the laundry
is clearly a sacrament.
A communion between the dirt of the world,
our hands, and an outcome
which we can predict
though not with certainty.
The shirt which has been washed a hundred times
inexplicably shrinks.
The socks are famed
for their lack of fidelity.
There is only so much we can do. ◉

SINUS INFECTION

I lie here and visualize
the healing vapors of antibiotic
wafting through my sinuses.
Not so much like an invading army
come to slaughter the multitudes of bacteria
who are squatting there
but rather more like a great spiritual teacher
who inspires the masses
to pack up and seek a new home, a better home,
someplace else.

It will take some pretty fancy doing
because, really, why should these bacteria
leave their warm safe home
and don't they, like most beings,
only want to settle down and be happy,
to go forth and multiply, to watch
their children and grandchildren
and great-grandchildren and so on and so forth
thrive and multiply as well?
There are many generations in my sinuses.
They have set down roots, their poets
have written many sagas about their lifetimes
of family dramas, the chaos of overcrowding.

Maybe the antibiotics
will be like Moses.
Maybe the neti pot
will be like the Red Sea.
Oh, neti pot! Oh, neti pot!
I rub the genie lamp shape of you
that you will grant my wish.
That you send forth floods.
That you will be
the Red Sea that does not part.
That you will be
a mighty river
that carries the colonies in little boats
led by their prophets
to a promised land on the other side
of me. ◉

AFTER SURGERY

The drugs play tricks on me.
I move my head fast and my stomach
does a hundred handstands,
each one kicks me hard.
It's almost a week of nausea now
and, though most everyone has endured worse,
I think I should at least
get a spiritual revelation out of the whole thing.
The retching and heaving leave me
feeling as hollowed out as those graceful bones
in the Georgia O'Keeffe documentary.
Everything she says is profound.
She is like an angel—she makes
no sudden movements to startle my stomach.
I take the bones of my fingers and form them,
still covered in flesh and blood,
into a telescope to the sky,
sky as blue as the ones in her paintings.
She sees life in her bones.
I still see death in mine.
Her ninety-something wrinkles seem younger
than anything about me right now.
But then, at the edges of my peripheral vision,
flowers,
so many flowers. ◉

FENCES

The eighteen-wheeler sound
is really the wind
rolling over
like the dreams that blow
through my sleeptime, filled
with important images
that I do not understand.
The eighteen-wheeler sound
is really the raven
winging by
bringing me the magic
I only half believe in.
A fence-sitter between worlds
I am swept up
in this bridge of sound,
follow the dreamtime images,
thumb a ride
with that raven,
offer my fences to the wind. ◉

VENUS IN RED COWBOY BOOTS

after a fiber art piece by Jo Wood, *Venus in Red Boots*

Venus in red boots
is clearly ready
to kick some serious ass.
These boots are made
for way more than walking,
will significantly raise the bar
for frolicking.
They exude a subtle fragrance
of strawberries and sex.

When Venus prances through the garden,
red dress in one hand
opulent pearl in the other,
butterflies alight in her hair.
Everything bursts into bloom.

When Venus throws
that alchemistic orb
which, like her, was born
in a foamy turbulent sea,
I chase it like a steamy future.
I am reborn in the running.

When I stop
in the petal-thick pinkly garden,
cherubs make smooth suggestions.
When I stop in the garden
I hold out my hands
until the butterflies land there.
I hold out my hands until the butterflies
call me home.

Venus carries on, keeps
kicking up
her otherworldly dust.
If we're lucky
it gets in our eyes.
If we're lucky

it gets in. ◉

STRAWBERRY

If you are a strawberry
you offer your two scents
of new love
and the sunlight in July
effortlessly
to the wind.

If you are a strawberry
these sultry nights are the best
and those ants,
with their tiny sensual feet
rubbing all over everything,
are your best friends.

If you are a strawberry
you know that you are
as sweet as it gets,
that no one else is as juicy.
You know that everybody wants
to pick you, to dip you
in chocolate and nibble on you,
to roll you around on their tongue,
swallow and inhale you,
take you in completely. ◉

PERSONAL AD

Desperately lonely, hostile, attention-starved, cranky woman seeks lover or companion or some combination (does anyone really know exactly what the hell they are seeking?!). I am middle-aged and average looking (you have probably passed me on the street and not noticed), neither trim nor employed with no interest in becoming either, have a long history in psychological therapy and am currently seeking more. I will alternate between needy, clingy insecurity and belligerent independence with unpredictable and unreasonable demands for space. You will find this delightful. I am seeking someone who wants to join me in throwing breakables against cement walls and putting their fists through sheetrock ones. This is how I see our first date. A glorious collage of shatterings, a disaster without pretense. You are someone who understands that this love affair like all love affairs is doomed to end in pain and agony the details of how exactly this will happen we cannot predict; we can only know that it will be terrible, will break whatever is left of our hearts. You are someone who will grasp and memorize every moment that doesn't suck and if we are lucky some parts of our encounters will not suck. I said if we are lucky. You understand that we probably won't be lucky. You are someone who will hear my stories and see the unmistakable way they point to the likelihood that touching me at all will bring you bad luck. You will find this charming. Your ghosts and mine will keep each other company—you and I will finally get some sleep. You will join me in emerging from a cocoon to become the moths that we are (no butterflies need respond) and fly, eyes wide open, into the nearest porch light. You will be able to eat the sweet strawberries dipped in the sugar and ground glass of our love. Intestinal fortitude required. You are fantasizing right now about taking me parking. ◉

PARKING ON SKYLINE PARKWAY

The lights of the city lay at our feet
like shells scattered on a beach,
like Liberace shrugged,
like every crow's deepest desire.
The moonlight on the water shimmers
like moonlight on the water.
We are parked with the engine off,
a nod to the disruptive power of carbon monoxide.
We do not want to be interrupted.
Our lips slide across each other's
like skinny dippers parting the surface
before immersing. Inquisitive fingers
ask a million questions
all of which are answered by ragged breathing.
Outside, other cars drive by,
shooting stars through the steamy windows,
indistinct and romantic until the police arrive. ◎

UNDER YOUR SKIN

I want to get under your skin
not exactly like scabies
but so you notice.
I want you to be a porter
with a genuine interest in baggage.
Mine is not made of canvas—
animals were hurt, blood was spilled.
I want you to have baggage of your own,
want us to inspect each other's entrail-covered cases,
to read them like tea leaves,
like poems in a foreign language.
I want to get into your system
not exactly like a tapeworm
but noticeably lodged and nourished,
the way some say love makes you insatiable
but doesn't weigh you down. I say
that love is as much a tapeworm as anything,
digesting the sweet meals
which we are so glad to feed it,
consuming everything that comes in.
I want you to invite me
on that slow drive to distraction,
to glory, to ruin,
to just drive
and to drive. ◎

I RIDE GREYHOUND

because it's like being
in a John Steinbeck novel.
Next best thing is the laundromat.
That's where all the people
who would be on the bus if they had the money
hang out. This is my crowd.
Tonight there are cleaning people appalled
at the stupidity of anyone
who would put powder detergent
into the clearly marked LIQUID ONLY slot.
The couple by the vending machine
are fondling each other.
You'd think the orange walls
and fluorescent lights
would dampen that energy
but it doesn't seem to.
It's a single's scene here on Saturday nights.
I confide to the fellow next to me
that I suspect I am being taken in
by the triple loader,
maybe it doesn't hold any more
than the regular machines
but I'm paying an extra fifty cents.
I tell him this meaningfully
holding handfuls of underwear.
He claims the triple loader
gives a better wash.

I don't ask why,
just cruise over to the pop machine,
aware that my selection
may provide a subtle cue.
I choose Wild Berry,
head back to my clothes. ◉

A DATE IS THE OBLONG FRUIT OF THE PALM

The dictionary defines dateless
as too ancient to be dated,
having no date, endless.
I want a date, have a hankering
for that particular sweet.
But there are no date-growing trees
on my landscape,
the soil I have
does not sustain them.
My palms grow
lines and lines of stories
but no dates. ◉

THE PHARAOH'S RHUBARB

The giant leaves,
filled with the rumors of poison,
could have served as fans for Cleopatra
had her barge floated down the Mississippi
instead of the Nile.
She would have loved rhubarb
with all of its barbarian associations
and questionable history, the intrigue
as to whether it should be trusted
as a fruit or as a vegetable.
Not even Cleopatra could defeat
her penchant for the bad boy.
And if that barge
floated her to current times on the Mississippi
she might be on a casino cruise
looking at brochures, her eyes drawn
to the red carpet unfurling to Caesar's Palace.
If Cleopatra were on that boat in Minnesota
she would be having a little lunch
or maybe a cappuccino with her rhubarb crisp.
Yes, she would be thinking about rhubarb
right before she gambled her future away
on a pair of snake eyes,
the bittersweet
lingering on her tongue. ◉

◎ TWO

Let's face it. We're undone by each other. And if we're not, we're missing something. If this seems so clearly the case with grief, it is only because it was already the case with desire. One does not always stay intact.

—Judith Butler

SNOW POEM

This is the kind of snow
which most reminds me of you.
I shovel under the moonlight
and feel you close.
Your memory keeps me
warm enough that these tears don't freeze
into something permanently
cold and hard.
Your memory keeps them
a warm river on which I can keep
hearing your voice, a river
with stories and waltzes and fish
of its own.
While I shovel
I know that you read me
as I type in this new language
"Sweet dreams, dear friend,
sweet dreams." ◉

NOTE

Sometimes I am still surprised
that you do not call, pissed
that you send no emails.

The trouble with the dead
is that they stay dead.
They consistently fail to show up
for even a single cup of coffee.
Sometimes

I think you are still
at home in England.
I want death to be like England—
you go there for awhile
but then you come back. ◉

BECAUSE THEY KNOW

The slant of light somehow
makes it feel like Christmas.
It's the 25th
but April, not December.
Still, somewhere today in Bethlehem
a Palestinian woman and an Israeli woman
are giving birth
against a backdrop of gunfire,
of wise men who have gone crazy,
of angels who have lost their way.
These women will weep for joy
at the absolute perfection and beauty
of their sons, they will weep in gratitude
that they have survived
this difficult birth.
They will weep because they know
that this boy
could break their hearts,
could be in the wrong place at the wrong time,
could someday lie as cold and pale in their arms
as this fresh shroud of snow,
could be sacrificed
for everyone else's sins. ◉

CHRISTMAS EVE

Christmas Eve and the highway
is lined with dead deer.
Here and there strings of light
are strung up against the dark,
some visceral impulse towards light.
An impulse which did not work out well
for those deer who never stood
a chance against the lights
that came for them.

Somewhere there are bombs
bursting in air—filling the sky
with light.

Somewhere else
a living child, unmaimed
and possibly well-fed,
is singing "Silent Night"
holding a lit candle
in a hopeful hand.

Here we are expecting snow.
Snow which will fall and fall
and cover every broken thing.
Will cover every broken thing
with a light blanket
for a little while.

Under the snow
deer eyes
keep watch through the night. ◉

THINGS MY FAMILY TAUGHT ME

If the armies come through
and beat you and rape you
and take everything you have,
you can make note of the fact
that it will be easier now
to keep the place tidy.

If you are in a camp,
drink the coffee grounds
as they will help you avoid parasites.
Keep a handful of pepper
to throw into the eyes of the guards.
If they give you a broth
and you are weak from every kind of hunger,
go to the edge of the fence
to where there is still some grass.
Reach your hand through
and pick a few blades of green,
arrange them in your soup.
Your eyes eat too
and they are as starved
as the rest of you.
Sing if you know to,
sometimes you will get extra water.
My grandfather kept
a small group alive this way.

Never become apathetic to politics,
to the erasures of small human dignities,
they are the bricks which will build the ovens.
Avoid the patriotism that turns the flag
into a blindfold and a whip.
Take a larger view and remember
that the victors write the history books.
Read between the lines.

It is possible to watch
women be raped until they die,
to step over dead bodies
and to somehow adapt
and if you can live through that
you can live through anything.
Appreciate every moment
when that is not your life.

Always carry tissues and some mints.
Offer sandwiches if someone
is going on a trip
because you never know
if the next place has food or not.

Never waste anything.
Remain belligerently optimistic. ◎

WALKING

A Tibetan prayer wheel
turns and turns,
sends prayers to the universe
with every revolution.
And now it is my feet,
all our feet,
walking,
one foot then another,
over and over,
every step a prayer
to stave off the horror
at the edges of our stomachs.
Every step a prayer.
One for the young man murdered,
one for each of the killers,
one for the people
who drove past the intersection
and did not stop,
one for me and the hope
that I would not do
the same thing.
Every step a prayer.
One for the woman found
long dead in a house
not far from me,
one for her killer,
one for the others
who beat her.
Every step a prayer.

One for the woman shot down,
one for the neighbors
who heard the shots
and did not respond,
one for me and the hope
that I would not do
the same thing,
one for the husband
who pulled the trigger
over and over.
Every step a prayer.
One for the people
who are buying a gun.
Who are buying a gun
because enough is enough,
because the prayer of walking
over and over together
is too slow
and the chamber of a gun
keeps on turning
sending its message to the universe.
It tells the lie
that this is the answer,
that what goes around
comes around
through its barrel.
A gun demands a sacrifice,
an enemy,
the willingness to kill.

A gun says follow me
and I will keep you safe.
I will be there
when you need me.
I will be there
when you think you need me.
I will be there
when you are not sure
but something happens fast,
I will be there.
Ask the questions later.
Better yet
don't ask the questions at all,
just buy a gun.
Shoot first and join in the prayer
of the chamber spinning and spinning,
that metallic prayer
that stops the feet from moving.
That stops the feet
from sending the prayers of movement,
of walking together,
one foot then another,
every step a prayer
to stave off the horror.
Every step a prayer
of walking together,
walking together,
walking together,
walking together. ◉

IN ITS TIME

In its time all things will be revealed
but revealed to whom?
In its time the Model-T was a great car
and it still is
but for different reasons.
In its time the lion will lay down with the lamb
but what will they dream about?
In its time the baby will be thrown out
with the bathwater
and will be very pruney,
grateful for a towel.
In its time the kitchen will be filled
with the bounteous smells
of supper in the oven.
In its time the dishes will be done.
Two plus two equal four
but someday they will equal five.
In its time justice will be served
with rolls and mashed potatoes. ◉

STAR

When I was little
I often wished on satellites.
Thought they were stars
shooting across the sky,
my wish in tow, messengering it
to the proper authority.
I have tried to learn astronomy,
to be one of those people
who can look up
and connect the dots
without the aid
of the planetarium staff.
I try but it is no use.
I see dippers all over the sky.
I see constellations everywhere
just never the same one twice.
Every night is a different show.
Every star a star in its own right
letting me watch,
small and grateful,
wishing on whoever is out there. ◉

BIRTHDAY POEM

A spiral is a candle
is a strand of DNA a
genetic predisposition
to ascension, is a
winding staircase climbing
to an understanding
of circles, of love
that keeps coming around
day after day,
season after season,
of a ring of friendship
of the brightness and
the warmth of a flame
of a candle whirling
around to another year,
another birth,
a burning spiral of time. ◉

FOREVER

I run my fingers through forever.
I feel the silk of it, the way it moves
fluid like a river.
I can tell that it's perfectly safe.
It is as graceful as that waltz
I always meant to dance,
as smooth as beach stones.
Forever is a series of random moments,
a glance of true recognition
or the way a hand
can tenderly touch a cheek.
When I touch your hair
it feels like forever.
Forever is breathing in
the sweet of hyacinths
and the summer promise
of peonies and lavender and thyme.
It's breathing out the aroma
of decaying autumn leaves,
the knowledge of the pure ice
and quiet snow to come.
Forever is the softest sort of summer rain
where my soulmate—
who has finally bothered to show up—
takes my hand
and we go for a walk.

I run my fingers through forever
and it is damp and mossy
with tiny wildflowers here and there
and there like here you can miss them
if you don't look closely enough.
Forever is that sand
that slips through my fingers,
that the water pulls suddenly from the shore
and sweeps away
down the wild wild river of itself. ◎

LILY

The throat of that lily
is impossibly deep
for that hummingbird.
Somewhere
a lover sighs. ◉

RIVER

I want to swim
in the long dark river of your hair,
want to rub up against
your smooth stones,
your secret mossy places.
I want our tongues to entwine
like strands of DNA,
to speak to each other
in a juicy language
that has not been
invented yet.
I want to absorb
the steady beat
in the timbre of your voice,
to be moved by the currents,
the cadences, the way
they toss me tempestuously
into complicated waters
until I am adrift
in what sometimes
feels like home. ◉

LONG DISTANCE

I am wondering if ghosts
maintain an interest
in sex.
I unbutton my blouse
in front of your picture,
unhook my bra,
unzip my pants.

I hope you are watching,
your cock rising.
I hope your ethereal lips
and agile tongue
still have an interest
in the raspberry nipple
I offer,
hope they can still
find that sweet. ◉

COMMUNION

The pale full moons
which cover the raspberry plants
are tinged with those first streaks of red
from the morning sky
before they emerge,
full fire suns shining sweetness
into the air and across my lips.
Everything is warm and lush.
I fill this blue bowl
with juicy red.
Summer drips its life blood
over my fingers
and down my throat. ◉

YOU CAN HEAR YOUR OWN MESSAGE IN A SHELL AND MAYBE IT'S THE SAME AS THE ONE I WANT TO SEND YOU...

Red earth shore embraces
flowing blue,
blue that can do
nothing but keep moving,
seek out and settle in the deepest place.

What message would I etch
onto a shell for you to find?
A watery one

of roots that get cut
but the trees stay alive,
trees that lean towards the water
in spite of opposing winds,
of that same wind that rustles our hair
though we stand on opposite shores,
of red clay earth
wrapping around
ever mutable blue. ◉

AND THE WATER WRAPS

I tell the Lake my life,
the ups and downs
and slow undulations.
It always listens
always comes back for more
even when the story is old
and it has heard it before.
Even when it comes in waves
one image at a time
and I can't describe
why they are important.
The Lake doesn't ask questions
because its story
comes in waves, too.

Swimming and the water wraps
around me, fills in
all the spaces that were me.
Each stroke glides out
a story and the Lake fills in
the hole I leave behind.

On the beach and the dunes
are a body full
of all those curves
I love to curl up into—
the part of the body
where ribs sink
into waves of hip, the crooks of arms.
I am nestled into the dunes
telling my life to the Lake
with sand in my teeth. ◉

SHE TURNS HER HEAD

She turns her head
and the city drowns in moonlight.
She turns her head
and remembers when she was a woman.
She places her hands, fingers spread wide,
against the frosty pane, studies
the prints her palms leave,
the way small rivulets of water
run down the stories of her lifeline.
She turns her head
and remembers a time when her chest didn't hurt.
She turns her head
and can't tell if she hears
the river or the wind rushing rushing
always rushing around her. She calms herself
by looking for bits of shell and driftwood,
leaves and feathers,
trinkets the elements leave behind.
She turns her head
and the colorwheel of beads
rolls off the table,
scatters baubles to the corners of the universe.
She turns her head
and the morning glories are blooming,
the lilies fold in on themselves
maples singe the cool blue,
then Christmas lights, then daffodils.

She turns her head
to the tulips, to the berries
to the tomatoes and to
the mysterious virus that kills them all
just before the ripening.
She turns her head
and watches the deer placidly gnaw
on what is left in the garden.
She turns her head
and the morning glories are blooming again.
She turns her head
and the big and little dippers
are flinging stars across the sky,
flecks of dust land in her eyes.
She turns her head
and follows the movements of the Northern Lights
before she falls into the darkness
they leave in their wake.
She turns her head
and the morning sky burns down the horizon. ◉

NEW GREEN

These are the last days
before the new green
darkens into summer
with its aching lush.
Apple blossom scent hangs
sultry in the humid air.
The ditches declare
a steady state of purple,
a shade which does not
suggest bruising.
I think about her—
fourteen, the click
of the institutional lock
punctuating our good-bye,
how the love of her family
is a rusty nail in her heart,
spiritual tetanus.
I watch her slide away
on the rivers
she carves into her skin,
into the new green of her life,
digging deep
into the heart of the life
she is sometimes trying
to live. ◉

HER EYES

one swollen black, rivet on him
when he enters the room.
Poolroom smoke a veil,
the eyes of the others a shield
between his fist and her body.
She clutches her pool stick,
a spear,
a modern day warrior.
But that is merely metaphor,
a wish for a weapon
she does not have,
has never had.
When he leaves she lets out
a long steady breath
and focuses her eyes,
one swollen black,
back on the eight ball. ◉

NANCY

I used to visit her
because she was my neighbor
and no one else ever did.
We would sit in her living room
where the drapes were heavy
and always pulled
against the natural light.
It was that stench
of unspecified and long-term despair
mingling with the booze and cigarette smoke,
which we took in with every breath,
into our lungs and hearts and other organs
while church music ground itself out in the
background.
She had one small lamp
with a stained and ruffled shade—
morning sun pink she called it,
her own small and personal sunrise.
But the dominant and omnipresent light
was the blue from the television.
She would place her hands
onto the screen to make contact
with the preacher who was always there.
She slid her thin dollars
into the envelope
like they were making love,
like it was a sacred union
on its way to be blessed by that man,

hands raised,
coming for her,
for that envelope,
coming for her. ◉

TO LYDIA

This is the child
the little girl who drifts around in you.
You see her sometimes,
starlight on a river.
You follow the light,
then retreat. Most of us do.
She is the one who will take you
on an adventure.
She is the one who will carry you
and you will be refreshed,
baptized in innocence.
Your eyes deepen
and become pools of memory,
fish and agates in your peripheral vision.
Her river floats you
on seaweed dreams.
Starlight on a river
is only visible on a calm clear night.
Your days are changed by the flickering.
Those stars with their perennial lessons:
shine, reflect, flow. ◉

PATTY

Candy bars at the store
were forty cents except
for those on sale
which were two for eighty-nine
and even though the sale ones
were more expensive
I bought one anyway
because they were Nut Goodies
and Patty McKee always had them
in third grade and we would eat one
on the way home
from school and it was Patty
who had the Suzy Homemaker oven
in her garage and we would
bake cakes and warm our feet in it.
She had older brothers and sisters
who told her the facts
of life and she told me
the boy pees inside of you.
We figured they had lied
until we found page twenty-eight of The Godfather
which we read secretly in the garage
our feet in the oven
giggling so loud that eventually
her mom came out
and even back then
I thought Nut Goodie bars
were too sweet. ◎

BOB

This cold has been around for a long time. It has settled into my lungs, has made itself at home there. As far as I can tell, it plans to stay for the rest of my natural life no matter how much garlic or lemon juice I consume. At first I am annoyed but, being adaptable, I get used to the idea. I name the virus Bob. Maybe it won't be so bad having a roommate again because sometimes people who live alone for too long become peculiar, even strange. Perhaps Bob was sent to save me from taking too great an interest in acquiring a houseful of cats. It's not so quiet around here now—even my neighbor remarks that he hears me coughing in the night right through the walls of the houses. I simply laugh and say, "Oh, that was just Bob." I try to get used to Bob's quirks and preferences, but it's tiring to have him around all of the time and it's not long before we start fighting. I say, "If you're going to live here you're going to have to start washing a dish now and then, and I'm getting pretty sick of being the only one who ever cleans the toilet!" Bob says nothing, just makes me cough—he's monotonous that way, can't really carry his part of the conversation. Sometimes I loathe Bob and I sense that he loathes me, as well. I tell him, "Go already if you don't like me anymore!" But he never does. ◎

ARS POETICA

One thing I really love about poems
is that they never interrupt
and tune you out
mid-sentence,
mid-thought,
mid soul-wrenching revelation
to answer their cell phones. ◉

IT'S A DIFFERENT GAME
AT THE OLYMPICS

It's not based on trust
like it is here.
There are no steroid tests
at the Rhubarb Festival.
This, in spite of the fact that the size
of some of those leaves
could make a suspicious mind look twice
at the seemingly benign growers
and their allegedly good-natured
growing methods.

I, of course, have never
had such a cynical thought.
I'm just saying

that if we put our heads together
they would still not take up
as much room
as one of those leaves.

But this is a nice festival in Minnesota,
family-oriented and full of pie,
and everyone knows
that nothing truly bad can happen
in the presence of that many
baked goods.
Still,

even with my good-sense lulled
by post-pie narcotic contentment,
there's no escaping it—
those leaves are really really big.
Too big.
Really really
too big. ◙

◉ THREE

Whatever can happen just might.

—John Trudell

MUSEUM GUARD

It is his job, his duty, his charge
to guard the art.
All if it.
Even the Mounties
who never look like they need guarding,
clean shaven slayers of Indians,
making off with female bounty.
He doesn't like them.
They give him the willies, the creeps,
the heebie-jeebies.
He dreams of them on dark nights,
huge horses and Aryan riders
almost catch up before he wakes up,
gets ready for work
and has almost shaken the aura
when a tourist inevitably asks
"where are they kept?"
Mounty pilgrims, they come in droves.
But one day someone else asks.
It is not a tourist.
Painting restorer, she says
she is here to load them up.
All of them.

The woman and her crew
do not look like painting restorers
and he was not told about this.
His hand is on the phone to check it out
before it occurs to him
not to. Leave it to fate, to karma
to the giant art critic in the sky
he helps them load that truck
then goes out for a walk
dreaming of Ann,
of fishing, of how the clouds
gallop across the sky. ◉

LUCIEN'S BIRTHDAY POEM

Yes, a dandelion
because they are the flower
of wishes. You blow that ball
of seeds and the wind
carries them to the one
assigned to grant or reject.
And it's a good thing
that it's the dandelions
who have this power
because they are tough
and sometimes you have to be tough
to even remember
that you have any desires left at all,
to believe that even one
could be satisfied, would not turn
to an example of
"Be careful what you wish for,
it might come true."
Maybe that's exactly why
there are so many of them—
the universe giving us extra chances
to keep dreaming.
Each one an uprising,
a burst of color
in the cracks of our hearts,
sunrise
at an unexpected time,
in an unexpected place. ◉

THE OTHER POET

The poet explains exactly
what her poems are doing on a variety of levels.
I am jealously impressed.
My poems go places
but send no postcards—I have no idea
what they are doing. They do
whatever they want to.
I give them curfews
but they wake me in the middle
of the night, they interrupt meetings
and other situations where I have no time
for them. They hang on me
when I am on the phone.
They do not keep my secrets
and sometimes they lie.
They can be sullen and withdrawn
or explosively obscene.
I think my poems have problems with authority,
conduct disorders, attention deficit.
The other poet is like the parent
with the bumper sticker about their honor student
while I am speeding along
to get to the correctional facility
before visiting hours are over.
I try to give my poems direction.
They tell me they have cleaned their rooms
but we both know it's not true.
After all these years of therapy
we still don't understand each other.
I write a poem and think
"What the hell is that?!" ◉

MUSE

This is what you should know
when you think it is romantic
to be a writer.
When you think it is relaxing,
a hobby, a diversion.
You should know that the Muse
of Renaissance paintings,
ethereal, full of love and good will,
is like the first shot of heroin
or that exhilarating sentence
which lures you to the pyramid scheme
that ruins your life.
These Muses are imposters
and, if they do exist,
they are visiting other writers.
They do not visit me.
My Muse is more like a Dominatrix.
She comes to me even when i don't call,
especially when i don't call.
Comes to me at inopportune moments
to remind me my time
is not my own.
Her whip in hand,
a sharp word on Her tongue,
She beats me to a pulp
to submission to a quivering mass
of pathetic humanity—

"And you call yourself a writer," She says,
mocking the work of my soul.
The core of my being, She rips it out
holds it up
to the cold light of day,
to Her harsh inspection
and finds it wanting.
She does not let me off the hook.
i am not excused.
i am drug through the murk
the alley the underworld
and if She is feeling charitable
She will reward me
with a crumb, a compliment,
a brief caress across my welts,
a kind or wicked word,
a word. ◎

THUNDER

Thunder rolls over the May night.
At first I think it's someone
pounding on the door,
I think maybe a serial killer
or maybe you.
Something primal overrides
house and logic, window and bed.
When I go to check
there is no one there.
There is only the thunder moaning,
the lightning
throwing knives at the sky. ◉

THE EQUATOR IS ONLY
AN IMAGINARY LINE

My tears waited
until I was halfway around the world
to fall for you.
Now there is nothing left for falling.
I feel you in the wild thrashings of the ocean
and in the sun
as it crawls across my skin.
You are just under the surface
of my restless sleep.
I hear your ardent whispers
in these howling winds
that blow in my ears,
tell me stories
I cannot repeat. ◉

THE DARK HONEY

The dark honey of you
drips through my mind
thick and sweet
I lick it off of my fingers
feel it slide
over every part of me
then your warm tongue
and salty words
a secret recipe
just between us
every heavy drop
its own particular kind
fragrant feast. ◉

THE WHITE COTTON NIGHTGOWN

lies crumpled in a heap
on the bed.
A gardenia trimmed in lace,
it holds the scent
of sweet dreams
and earthy desires.
The temporary blossom floats
serene in a tangle
of turbulent blankets. ◉

CONFESSION

I used to feel lust
looking at pictures
of Jesus.
This is probably worse
than anything Freud
could have dreamed up.

It's not really surprising,
me focused
on some unavailable man,
someone clearly
out of my league.

At the time I was too young
to fully appreciate
all of the ramifications
though I did understand
that I should keep these thoughts,
like so many of the others,
to myself. ◉

IDLE HANDS ARE THE DEVIL'S WORK

Debbie does Dallas,
Duluth does Dylan,
Delia does the dishes.
Everyone is busy
doing something.
Except for me. ◉

QUAKER MEETING

I have come to Quaker Meeting because I like the idea of sitting quietly in a circle with people who are contemplating spiritual and nonviolent ways, to become centered and serene, but I notice that it isn't really quiet—there is traffic outside, people are downstairs having coffee—I would like some coffee—and others walk across the impossibly loud floorboards, they shift positions in creaking pews and I think about how Quakers always remind me a little of oatmeal and now I am thinking about oatmeal and of my suspicion that most truly good people eat oatmeal because it is so healthy and cheap and wholesome and I have tried to like it but stubbornly continue to hate hot cereal of all kinds, indicating that I'm probably not very good deep down inside and, as if to prove it, my mind wanders into that territory where you are never supposed to go when you are in church, and though the Quakers are likely more open-minded than the Lutherans on this topic, I'll bet they would say that Meeting isn't the place to be thinking about sex so, of course, it's all I can think about now and not the sweetly loving spiritually connected kind, no, I'm thinking about the fishnet-stockings-talk-dirty-fuck-me-now kind of sex, the very worst kind to be thinking about in church, the kind that gets you sent to hell in short order and the only other thought that enters my mind is that there are clearly some problems with my personality which reminds me about yesterday when I was talking with a friend whose very existence I was celebrating at his birthday party when he told me, "Go ahead and have the cheesecake because you are at the point in your life where, if you ever do date again, it will be because someone is interested in your personality." Hmmmm...my personality...very bad news...and here, in this quiet peace-loving circle, it occurs to me that I could put out a hit on him, take out a contract on his life, these things are probably done all the time, and though I have lived my life committed to pacifist ideals and he is a long-time friend who has a young child, this murder

84

for hire seems the only reasonable response and then I start to wonder about group rates because it's just like they say about that slippery slope, once you consider having one person killed, it's not much of a leap to start killing off others like the man who asked me when the baby was due when I was not pregnant—yes, he will have to go—and I suspect the Quakers aren't as big on hell as the Lutherans but they may have an emergency one for people who think about lewd sex and develop hit lists during Meeting so I try hard to think of something, anything else but am so spiritually small and shallow that I remember more people, more slights and insults and wonder if I should add them to the list but I find my bloodlust waning and I congratulate myself on this spiritual progress, this new-found lack of homicidal impulse and I almost laugh out loud but pull myself together enough not to and try to pay attention to the thoughtful and uplifting messages some of the others are moved to share but my back and neck are starting to hurt, I have to go to the bathroom, want to shift positions but am afraid of the thunderous pew creaking drawing attention to my degenerate self and finally it's over and someone good and glowing with pure and peaceful thoughts is inviting me downstairs but I don't go there. ◙

I WANTED TO WRITE A POEM
FOR THE 25TH ANNIVERSARY
OF THE WOMEN'S COFFEEHOUSE

And I wanted it to go way back
to when I first remember coming here,
when it was new and when the personal was political
and the peaceful revolution
was everywhere.

The poem would start with a presentation
about reclaiming women's health
via the vaginal self-exam.
It would have a mirror and a plastic speculum.
Barbie and Midge would saunter in,
first edition copies of *Our Bodies, Ourselves*
tucked under their arms.
They would definitely not
be wearing heels but maybe Earth shoes
or hiking boots.
They would have on T-shirts and buttons
that said, "War is Not Healthy for Children and
Other Living Things," "Power to the People,"
"People Before Profit," "A Woman Without a Man is
Like a Fish Without a Bicycle,"
"Bread Not Bombs," and, my personal favorite,
which I can slip in because I am the one
writing the poem, "If I Can't Dance
I Don't Want to Be Part of Your Revolution"
and they would mean every word of it.

They would do their best with those tiny speculums
and you might think
that the lack of genitals in the world of Barbie
would be a problem but
you would be wrong because these are
"Look At My Cervix" Barbie and Midge.
After the presentation
they would throw away their tampons
in favor of sea sponges, the bras already
a thing of the past.

The poem would have been
filled with witty dialogue
and insightful commentaries
about the women and the foibles
and the politics of the day
until, finally, at the end of the poem
(which would take a really long time
because nothing could end
until there was true consensus)
everyone would go downstairs
and dance. ◙

BARBIE GROWS ARMPIT HAIR
—for Linda

It was first noted
in the 7th aisle
of the Cash Is Ours toy store
by Madeline who was playing
with the demo model
and asked her mother
why Barbie had a moustache
under her arms.
The ensuing shriek
brought all three managers-on-duty
and an off-duty medic.

It all started with Belinda
who worked the night shift
in the Barbie and Friends
quality control section
of the factory.
She had worked there for years
checking countless heads
for misstamped eyes, crooked lips,
bad hair.
It was also her job
to administer a short verbal quiz
to make sure the Barbies
had right political beliefs
and Mattel family values.

All the subversives and socialists
were sent back.
Until one day
Belinda had been passed over
for yet another promotion
and the foreman asked her
to shorten her breaks
and smile more often.
In her irritated, distracted state
she let one of the feminist Barbies
keep talking and suddenly something
clicked.
Naturally it was only a matter of time
before she let through
Body Hair Barbie
and Menstrual Midge,
complete with tiny pad,
tampon, sea sponge, and ibuprofen accessories.
There was Softball Skipper
Bi-Barbie and Drag Queen Ken.
Some little girls
and some little boys
found their horizons broadened,
their lives irrevocably changed
before Belinda got fired. ◉

WINONA

Winona is Barbie's walleye warrior friend,
comes complete with a boat
and spearfishing equipment.
Mattel was proud of their attention
to ethnic diversity and affirmative action,
pretty pleased until they realized
she planned to fish on ceded territory,
had a copy of an old treaty
that said she could.
Free-thinking and liberal
until they noticed Barbie organizing
a witness program and offering convertibles
to anyone with a transportation problem
for free.
Mattel tried to get Winona
to abrogate by offering
bendable elbows and a boyfriend
but she said "No, thank you"
and Barbie watched
as they tried to pull Winona off the shelves. ◉

BARBIE DISAPPEARED ONE DAY

There was lots of speculation,
kidnap, foul-play
maybe a Jimmy Hoffa kind of thing.
The National Enquirer once linked them
in the exposé
"Where dolls and mobsters meet."
Actually, she just got sick
of the fame thing
and joined her real life lover
Elvis
who had been hiding out in Michigan
but had to move
once the tabloids found him.
Moved to Chicago
which is where Barbie found him
working as a roadie
for some of the local bands
and shooting up everything
he could melt down.
Eventually the needle found its way
to Barbie and the little-known vein
that ran up her plastic arm.
And that's how they lived and loved
on the lower east side,
closer to Jimmy than they thought
until they got busted
in a small-time liquor store hold-up.

Elvis escaped.
Barbie got sent downtown
where she confounded the authorities
by having no fingerprints,
aggravated the telephone operator
by insisting
that Midge and Skipper
didn't have any last names. ◉

VISITING VENUS

1.

It was Friday and Barbie was primping, getting ready to pay her annual tribute to Venus, the goddess of beauty and love. It was she who had bestowed the gifts of beauty and charm to Barbie at birth so she owed her. Barbie enjoyed these visits though she was never completely relaxed because she knew that Venus could be touchy and, when offended, well, let's just say Venus specialized in cursing the offender to various sexual perversions, none of them pleasant. People used to darken their windows when the light of Venus shone lest her planet make them sick. Barbie could see that. She was bringing apples and a silver handheld mirror for Venus to add to her collection.

2.

This year the visit was at Venusburg, the legendary cavern of sensual pleasure. She was all set to drive her convertible over but Venus insisted on picking her up in the swan-drawn chariot. Well la-di-da. Turned out the swan-drawn chariot was pretty cool.

3.

When they got to Venusburg they nestled into the overstuffed pink and red brocade chairs and enjoyed hot mugs of pounded poppies with milk and honey. "This is the same thing I drank on my wedding night," said Venus. "My dad arranged the marriage, you know. I would never have married Vulcan, the ugliest god ever, who was lame because his mother threw him over a balcony when he was a baby. Apparently it was a face even a mother couldn't love." Venus laughed. "Anyway, he had his good sides. He was god of the forge—big deal, right?—but he created great jewelry for me, and for a wedding gift—say, did you know that 'gift' is the German word for poison?—he made me a Magic Girdle." Barbie's ears perked up at the mention of jewelry and lingerie. "It's a gorgeous embroidered thing and whoever wears it cannot be resisted." "Isn't that an odd present for a husband to give a wife who is already irresistible?" Barbie asked. "He must have felt very secure in his manhood. Ken is like that, too." "Nah, Vulcan is just odd. I was clear with him from the get go that this would be an open marriage. And people think that idea came out of the 60s—ha! My affairs, I'm proud to say, are many and varied and legendary. Every woman should be so lucky."

4.

Venus modeled the Magic Girdle and, even though Barbie had no sexual organs, she felt something stir. "In your dreams," laughed Venus. The rejection stung. Barbie, after all, had her pride. She lashed out. "You're a slut!" Venus sighed. "How a word that basically refers to a woman who enjoys the pleasures of the flesh with a nice variety of partners became a put-down I will never know. I can't believe women go along with that crap. I'm the goddess of exactly that sort of thing—I encourage the meretricious many to carry deliciously on and on."

"Hadn't looked at it that way," Barbie begrudged and then got angrier the way people do when someone points out flaws in their theories. "All the venereal diseases of the world are named after you!"

"Shit happens, love hurts, grow up," Venus replied with a wave of her hand.

"I've got way better clothes than you except for your stupid old Magic Girdle! (and here Barbie felt a sharp pang of jealousy). I'm the new standard of beauty—you're nothing but an ugly old washed up has-been!" Barbie knew the minute it came out of her mouth that she'd gone too far.

"You've gone too far," said Venus with ice in her voice. "Just for that I'm not going to give you this replica of my Magic Girdle." And here Venus held up a perfect miniature of the enchanting garment. Had Barbie had any insides they would have been twisting in a thousand knots. "And," Venus continued, "you're also not getting those genitals you've been wishing for! Not now, not ever!" The walls of the cavern shook with the force of Venus's words.

5.

"Shit," Barbie thought on her long walk home. "Shit, shit, shit, shit." ◙

VENUS LIMERICK

—for Charles

There once was a goddess named Venus.
And I'll tell you something just between us,
She was familiar with Freud
Had a lot of sex she enjoyed,
But never once envied the penis. ◉

THE PRUNE KOLACHI

The call of the prune kolachi
is not audible to everyone.
It only arrives, pitch perfect
and elegantly enunciated,
to some of us,
to those of us with
ears finely tuned
to the siren songs of baked goods.
The Bake Shoppe in New York Mills
is my current Mecca,
my daily pilgrimage. The need
for the kneaded and unkneaded alike—
a metaphor for equanimity
toward all of humanity,
toward all things seen and unseen.
The kolachi is baked
for the good and evil alike.
It is a testament to faith
in the sweet singing fruits and grains of creation.
I take and eat.
I testify and hum praises under my breath.
I listen for the voices
of angels. ◎

THE MYTH OF SOLID OBJECTS

I can't tell
if this burning in my chest
is heartache or heartburn.
This distracting fire
confuses a distinction
between solid and ethereal.
Some physicists say
there is no difference,
that when matter is broken down
into its smallest part
it is actually a wave
which explains the phenomenon
of holding on to something
to someone for dear life,
then feeling them slide away,
your hands empty,
players in the myth of solid objects.
So little can be held.
The memory gets fuzzy,
the piano won't hold its tune,
time runs out
for a singer holding a note.
You cannot hold me,
I cannot hold that thought
yet it stays,
some belligerent thing
interfering with the flow
of blood and stomach acid.
I am filled with water and fire,
two ideas which everyone knows
cannot mix. ◉

IN 1986 THE RADIO REPORT

comes while I am at work stuffing futons
and selling earrings while Chernobyl
spews destruction. The radio drones
surreal with unsubstantiated death
tolls and the cloud moves West
to where Herta's arthritic fingers play Schubert
and Fritz picks stinging nettles for their tea.
West to my aunts who clean real and imagined dirt
with all the vengeance of their war shattered pasts,
where Gisela has just built a house with her lover
and Ulrike is beginning to discover boys.
The announcer is relentless
and the person who has been asking me questions
about how to keep their futon clean
has finally wandered off to find another clerk
and I am outside on a balmy April sidewalk
that leads to the Hacienda and a table of friends.
I join them and keep ordering beer
not knowing what that cloud is doing
while I am at this table
with people who can change the subject
because Fritz never made them tea, my aunts never
scrubbed their perfectly clean socks and they never
made Ulrike blush by telling her how pretty she is
and finally I am too drunk to call Germany, too drunk
to talk or cry but not drunk enough
to forget the sonatas that waft from Herta's piano. ◉

CROW

Out in the street
I hit a crow with my car
and the crow dies.
I call for a moment of silence.
My niece asks, "Why?
It was just a crow
and we have to go
to the Cities and where
could that crow have been going
that is more important
than that?" ◉

FLUSHING FLUSHING FLUSHING
ALL ACROSS AMERICA

...our toilet is really a drag because every time you flush it the little chain that connects the handle to the plunger falls off and you have to reach your hand way down into the tank, way down into the freezing cold water and reconnect everything and while I'm reaching and reconnecting I think about millions of other people flushing their shit into a lake and about fish choking on all that shit and about places where people don't have enough water even to drink and here we are flushing flushing flushing all across America while the aquifers are running dry and there is talk of piping water from Lake Superior to Texas and by the time I have everything reconnected my fingers are numb from the cold... ◙

SWIMMING

Yes, it is a lovely room,
lovelier before the ceiling
let down sheets of itself
alerting us to the fact
that the kids had made
a swimming pool for Barbie
up in Megan's room.
It would have been fine
and we encourage creative play
and a cardboard box
can be a lot of different things
but it doesn't make
a good swimming pool
unless the water is pretend
which was not the case.
No, this pool featured real water
and Barbie loved it,
floating the dead man's float
under the glow of the overhead light,
turning every now and then
her beautiful hair flowing
like Ophelia drifting downstream,
trying to get to the living room. ◎

TURTLES

The box of Turtles sits
unpurchased on the counter.
I want them
so I recite my list of reasons
to leave them, to walk away
and not look back.
Fattening.
Obviously.
All those cashews and aren't those
nuts of oppression
which we are boycotting in solidarity
with someone somewhere?
The caramel would surely
rip this temporary crown
right out of my mouth and let's not forget
the level of pain my tooth and I endured
before it became royal.
I have just enough money
to buy a birthday card for my aunt
and to take the bus home.
On my walk home it begins to rain
and I think as soon as I finish
this last one I could maybe put the box
over my head like a little hat. ◉

TEETH

I.
Teeth are the tiny mountain ranges
in my mouth. Eyetooth peaks, mesas,
saw tooth molars, mother lodes of silver.
Plants and animals fluctuate.
My fingers and the floss around them
are the forest rangers
keeping down populations,
causing earthquakes and floods.

II.
There are shark teeth, buck teeth,
bear teeth, and the straight teeth
I'd give my eyeteeth for.
Crooked, broken, chipped, flossed,
and teeth with flecks of spinach.
Teeth fall out in dreams
and in age,
can live in a cup,
attract fairies. ◙

◎ FOUR

I have woven a parachute out of everything broken.

—William Stafford

JOYCE

Humid air hangs syrup thick
with the smell of peonies,
ripe as this picture
of Joyce nude.
Full moon belly and lush breasts,
she is a tropical forest
about to rain milk. ◉

MAGDA

I.

You are not in many
family pictures. Only two
out of the fifty-some
in front of me.
One is a family portrait.
You are a young woman
and the only one
whose eyes are not
looking at the camera.
Yours are slightly
to the left,
a little too wide.
They say you had visions
and fits and no amount
of church could make you stop.
My grandmother says
you were deranged.
Townsfolk thought
you were possessed
or had relations
with the devil.
My grandfather says
you were a whore,
had relations with everyone
especially the hangman
who was the son
of the minister,
brother of the judge

and the only reason
you were alive at all.
In 1908 your village
still believed in witches
and this fear kept
the midwife and the doctor
away while you labored
and labored, birthed
yourself and your child
to another world.
The second picture
is you in a casket—
some family member's
final test—
would you show up
on film?
You are holding
a swaddled bundle
and your eyes
are open and steady.
They said they tried
to keep them closed.

II.

They called me whore
and witch but I say
I was their mirror.
They took their turns with me
then went home

pious and throwing stones.
Home to their wives
who came to me in secret
when one more mouth
would have been too much
to bear.
I lived on the outskirts
with all the plants
and I learned their virtues,
this one to take
a fever,
that one
a baby,
the other to calm
the spirit.

I met the hangman
in the small clearing
past the river bend.
He sat still as the stone pile.
I thought it was an altar
but he would never say,
only that they always asked
something special at the end.
"Tell Anna I always loved her."
"Don't forget me in your prayers."
And he never did
forget any of them,
they were his only companions

before me.
One day
when we were both
particularly young
we were walking
and happened upon
the minister in the act
of knowing his daughter.
We stood and bore
unrelenting witness,
no amount of pleading
would take our eyes
off of him.

Later,
when the movement was afoot
to put me to death,
the minister told the townsfolk
an angel had visited him,
instructed them to let me live
as an act of Christian charity.
Sometimes they left food
but we never ate it.

They could never look at me
because I had seen them all.
My vision
was my power. ◎

LIGHTNING

Razor blade lightning slices open
the wrists of the night sky.
For once
an appropriate gesture.
And now finally,
standing here in the rain,
some peace. ◉

LIPS

The smooth way the wind
has turned the snow,
the folds of curtain
with their teasing billow,
full undulating swells of waves
all mystery and life force
hidden from view.
Everything reminds me of your lips.
Everything curved and graceful
fills me with surprise
that I had not noticed them before. ◉

A DISTRACTING THOUGHT

The other night
I meant to offer you
a ride home.
But then you hugged me
and I got distracted
by your warm neck
and the way it made me want
to take you home with me.
I forgot about the ride
but I remember about your neck—
my nose and lips
pressed up against it,
wanting to
stay there longer,
to see where that
could take us. ◉

INTO SUMAC

I want to take you down
into sumac dreams
pungent and softer,
to fill a basket with bells
and peal away walls.
I want to go to the river
and swim into your sleep,
float in moonwater, trust
no monsters will pull me under. ◎

AWAKE

My heart is awake.
Its eyes open,
its arms spread wide,
legs, too.
Ridiculously open to you.
Absurd valentine
caught
on the underbelly
of your soul.
Unnoticed on the sole
of your shoe.
Still my heart
goes with you. ◎

LAST WORDS

You were a flame
that I flew into.
Now I am
the underachieving cousin
of the Phoenix,
a pile of ashes
who will not rise again.

It's not a dream exactly
but I can hear you tell her
how I mean nothing to you,
how not even the smallest light
is left on for me
in any window of yours.

At my funeral
not a single person
will be able to say:
"She was nobody's fool." ◉

ON SENDING YOU
A BLANK SHEET OF PAPER

It's my best poem.
It's that silence of which we spoke,
that truth forever hiding
between the lines—now
it has the whole page to itself.
It's everything you want to know.
It's everything I need to tell.
It explains in meticulous detail
how I learn about love by the scent
it leaves as it walks out of the room,
the way I learn about death
by staying alive.
Nothing I can say is relevant.
But you can read all of that and more
on that blank page—finally
the whole story.
It's a song I wrote for you
with perfect phrasing and pentameter,
absolutely in tune with the rhythms
of all of the emptiness which surrounds it.
It's the perfect love letter—nothing
to offend or misinterpret or disappoint.
It's my best poem.
Everything I have,
I send it to you. ◉

JESUS RISING

I watched Jesus rise
up the side of the Damiano Center on 4th Street.
Ropes and pulleys hoisted
the fisher of men into the air,
hands outstretched and open.

His face and robes glow
with fresh paint as per Historical Society specs.
He is compelling and benevolent looking
though terribly pale,
elegant in this neighborhood full
of broken glass and boarded up windows.

I watched Jesus rise
and thought about loving everybody
even the seagulls
who are the agreed-upon enemy
in this city, in spite
of the lilting way they fly
or how their songs complement the waves
drumming the shore.

Right now all of the seagulls of the world
are in the Damiano parking lot,
some sort of miracle of bread,
Jesus smiling. Flecks of shattered glass
glint in the light of the sun. ◉

WATCHING

after a print by Gaylord Shanilec, *Watching*

The sunlight charms the leaf
out of its bud.
Pale green luminous cobra
with a walleye on its back,
it watches
the orderly and unorderly world
laid out at its metaphorical feet.
It slithers and swims into the light,
sways to the hypnotic pulse of the sun.
It keeps its eyes on something
we cannot yet see. ◉

REGARDING THE PRISONER
WHOSE NAME THE RADIO ANNOUNCER
SAID WAS NOT LISTED IN THE REPORT
AND WHOSE IDENTIFYING NUMBER
I DO NOT REMEMBER

The last thing the prisoner saw
before he died at Guantanamo Bay
was a military issue boot
coming at his head.
This is not a metaphor. This is
journalistic truth.
Well, at least the part about him
getting kicked to death.
I don't really know
if that boot
was the last thing he saw.
Maybe he was lying on his back
and could see the eyes
of his final assailant. Maybe
he was looking at the floor or the ground,
the ceiling or the sky.
Maybe he had his eyes closed,
the only act left
over which he had control. Maybe
he had his eyes closed and could see
the faces of his mother or his father
or his child or his truest love or his closest friend.

Maybe he saw the landscape of his homeland
and the way the colors
of the sky at dusk
always made everything so beautiful,
so much more beautiful
than anything he had ever seen
here. ◎

THE MOURNING AFTER THE SCHOOL SHOOTING AT RED LAKE

This morning
every tuft
of crumpled grass
is a nest—
empty
and filled
with sorrow. ◙

THE HANDS OF TIME

Everything moves
at the speed of a lily
and every day a million snowflakes melt
on somebody's tongue.

The hands of time travel
across my skin
and deliver their holy benedictions.
I keep living in this world
without a reference point.

At night I lay my head on my pillow,
my pillow that is filled with feathers,
filled with the ephemera of flying.
When I close my eyes
a hundred birds
sing me to sleep. ◙

LAST GOLD

The last gold
leaves the trees
naked and alone.

I pack away
all my pictures
of the dead.

The last red leaf
drops from the maple.

A million hands reach out
to each other
and to nothing. ◎

THE HANDS

The hands of the enemy
are the same
as the hands of a friend,
same muscles contracting, same
nerves conducting, same
metacarpals rippling.
Some of the fingers
have rings which tell a story
about a heart. The heart
of the enemy is the same
as the heart of a friend,
same vivid blood passing through
one red chamber, then another,
every room filled
with a thousand stories
all waiting to be told, one hand
offering the other
fruit and bread. ◉

PATRIOTISM

My country is this dirt
that gathers under my fingernails
when I am in the garden.
The quiet bacteria and fungi,
all the little insects and bugs
are my compatriots. They are
idealistic, always working together
for the common good.
I kneel on the earth
and pledge my allegiance
to all the dirt of the world,
to all of that soil which grows
flowers and food
for the just and unjust alike.
The soil does not care
what we think about or who we love.
It knows our true substance,
of what we are really made.
I stand my ground on this ground,
this ground which will
ultimately
recruit us all
to its side. ◉

WINTER BABY

I may not know who I am but I know where I'm from.
—Wallace Stegner

I am from the dead,
the dead of winter
where only our stories
keep us warm.
I am from the low groan
of ice heaving over the swells
of the coldest lake on earth.

I'm from the first line of red
that slices along the horizon
separating day and night.
I'm from those red clouds
that only stay a little while.

I'm from the crunching sound
the snow makes when you walk on it
at twenty below zero, the deep creak
of the wooden stairs,
the way everything is on the verge
of shattering.

I'm from the huge snowdrift
packed hard with snowplow ice
cascading down the steps,
I'm from the way the moonlight shines on
everything while I'm shoveling.

I'm from the feel of the muscle
behind my shoulder blade
when I am done.

I am from thirty below zero
with added windchill factors,
from where the most banal accomplishment
becomes heroic, where every breath
fuses the nostrils.

I'm from mittens that need darning,
I'm from the bits of wool that almost match,
from the needle that blends the old and the new,
from a thousand other hands that have mended
a thousand other mittens.

I'm from the darkest time of the year,
the time full of candles and Christmas lights—
our modern solstice fires.
I am from the embers of those fires,
from the crackling hiss of blue heat,
from the spark that flies
into the night sky
and disappears. ◉

FROM THE DUST OF THE STARS

…from what we cannot hold the stars are made.
—W. S. Merwin

Before the stars were fully formed,
before whatever makes up the substance
of stars was being invented by the universe,
flecks of the idea of you and of me were there,
commingling.

I have always loved you.
The pre-star dust of you fills my cells.
There is nothing I can do.

When I touch you I touch everything
from before the beginning to after the end.
I look into the dark night of your eyes
and see a sky full of stars,
all of them filled with an eternity of wishes
shooting through the heavens
light-years and lifetimes away. ◉

IF I WERE THE MOON

If I were the moon
I would turn your tide.
You would draw maps of me,
would want to learn everything
about my topography,
you would lick me to see
if I am made of green cheese or not.
You would memorize the names
of my mountains and seas.
If I were the moon
you would watch for me,
you would study my face and my curves
and the way my movements
make shadow pictures on your walls.
If I were the moon
you would smile at me
and I would climb in through your window.
I would fill your room
with my own particular madness-inducing
lunacy-producing light.
I would shine on you and make you howl
until I could taste my name
on your lips and in your mouth. ◉

MAMMAL POEM

The meaning of life
is the way your tongue
circles my nipple,
then moves on to the rest
of the scorched earth of my body,
waters me with something
that could keep me alive.

I read that my clitoris
contains 8000 nerve bundles.
I have decided that I want you
to make love to each one
individually,
some of them
twice. ◉

LETTING GO

You come to visit me
and I let go
of every pretension.
I take them off
button by button
along with my blouse.
They fall away
and I meet parts of myself
no one could have predicted.

You unhook my bra
and my last inhibition.
I take off whatever you want.

You blow onto the embers
of a fire fueled
with the oldest sort of wood.
This is the kind of fire
that could lick you clean.

You leave your mark on me.
Even when you are not here
my fingers can see you in the dark. ◉

BLUE MOON SLEEP

lets in birds and water animals
that swim through secret skies
underground seas.
Lines that separate
elements dissolve
and everything is
undulating blue.
I am flying slow with the fish
and all the silvery creatures.
We ebb out new day tidings
through rivers and canyons
marvel and wonder
at the stalactites of the soul,
the midnight tides of indigo dreams. ◉

PORTENT

The moon shines seductively
on the new snow.
The corner streetlamp
provides a harsh counterpoint.
My tides are pulled
from one side to the other.
There are so many kinds of light.
But a shadow is a shadow—

same back alley of the soul every time.
I have acquired my own stoop here.
It's often quiet and contemplative,
my visitors—ephemeral, made up
of matter from other worlds,
parallel universes, scenes
from the old movies of my life
that play on a continuous loop.
The moon and the streetlight

are equally round tonight.
They are two crystal balls
spilling my secret possible futures
as far as and farther
than I can see. ◉

THE AUTUMNAL EQUINOX

It's the time the Buddhists say
the veil between the living and the dead
is the thinnest.

The earth tilts the sky
to a deeper shade of blue,
turns all the leaves
to a million suns
rising and setting and swirling
in wild abandon all around us.
They are dervish dancers of coolness,
they spin for the long quiet ahead.

Your mother comes to sit with you.
My lover runs his tongue
along my shoulder blades.
Friends float in and sniff our coffee,
they touch us lightly on our cheeks,
kiss our foreheads.

We walk out into the crisp
of the world we are still in,
feel a foreign wind
at the nape of our necks.
The earth tips,
curtains billow and wave,
leaves twirl by. ◎

SNOW BLIND

Winter arrives
with its icy brilliance,
with its layers
and layers of snow
holding the silences
in its own geology of quiet.
Every flake that falls
is a diamond
that cuts and exposes
the essential until I am
snow blind to most of the world
except for the impossible blues
in the sky and in my bones,
except for the dazzling
bewildering light.
Even when I close my eyes
I can see the sun.
I can see the sun. ◉

TAKING IT OFF

Some years are just
one hair shirt layered onto another,
each one doing its best
to fuse with skin.

Now is the time
I will finally peel them off,
a slow psychological striptease.
I examine each one only briefly
then throw it
onto an enormous fire,
that original bonfire
fueled by grace and forgiveness,
by the bones
of a thousand other troubles.
Its tongues of flame
sing torch songs and the blues, praises
for every dull, flawed, and disastrous thing.
Its flames lick and illuminate wounds,
leave smoke and spark and new mirrors.

Finally the last one comes off.
I stand here
naked and perfect,
just like you,
just like everyone. ◙

About the Author

Ellie Schoenfeld is a poet native to Duluth, Minnesota. She is the author of two previous poetry collections, *Screaming Red Gladiolus!* (Poetry Harbor, 1999) and *Difficult Valentines* (Fallow Deer Books, 2004), and her work has been published in an anthology, *The Moon Rolls Out of Our Mouths* (Calyx Press, 2005), with the four other women in her writing group. Schoenfeld enjoys collaborating with artists of other genres. Her work is featured along with the music of some of her favorite musicians on the CDs *Personal Ad*, *Almost Through the Rinse Cycle,* and *Taking It Off.* She has worked with area groups Poetry Harbor and Spirit Lake Poetry Series. Though she has thought about it extensively, she has never actually run away with the circus.

CPSIA information can be obtained
at www.ICGtesting.com
Printed in the USA
LVOW04s1008121216
516881LV00013B/138/P